Color Me
in
BASIC FALL SHIT

Fall Bucket List
Hayrides
CARVE PUMPKINS
GET LOST IN A CORN MAZE
Jump in the leaves
FOOTBALL
Trick-or-Treat
have s'mores & bonfire
Drink Apple Cider
Count Our Blessings

let there be
PUMPKiN SPiCE

autumn
breeze
and
pumpkins
please

Nuts
ABOUT
Fall

Forget your pumpkin spice.
Its Cider & Donuts
season

The
beauty
* OF FALL
COLORS

Bee grateful
HONEY

Autumn

flannels
bonfires
s'mores

you had me at
pumpkin
SPICE

bonfires
& boots

Fuck your pumpkin spice.
IT`S APPLE CIDER SEASON.

LET'S
DUMPKIN
Spice
things up

CAMPING
is
my
THERAPY

My favorite
COLOR
IS
OCTOBER

pumpkin spice
is my favorite
season

Hello
Autumn

pumpkin
spice
everything.

Autumn
IS MY FAVORITE
COLOR

Grab your Balls
Its canning season

happy
fall y'all

hello
Fall

thankful
grateful
blessed

FLANNELS
Pumpkin Patch
HAYRIDES
Caramel Apples
BONFIRES
Hot Chocolate

basic witch

THE LEAVES WILL SHOW YOU HOW BEAUTIFUL IT IS TO
let go

'TIS THE
season
TO BE
Basic

CRACKLING FIRES
crunchy leaves
hot coffee
CRISP MORNINGS
chilly nights
COZY SWEATERS
football
pumpkin everything

BOO
Happy Halloween

It's
FALL
Y'all

happy
Halloween

but i think
i love fall
most of all.

WE MAKE UP HORRORS TO HELP US COPE WITH

THE REAL ONES

Leaves
ARE
falling
Autumn
is
calling

FALL
pumpkin
leaves
everything
harvest
sweater weather

Sweater
WEATHER

PUMPKIN
spice life

I am wicked
in many ways

in a World
full of
Princesses
Be a
WITCH

trick-or-treat

grateful
thankful
blessed

thankful

grateful

thankful

blessed

let us be
THANKFUL